W9-BCC-598

What Happens at a
Museum?

By Lisa M. Guidone

Reading Consultant: Susan Nations, M.Ed.,
author/literacy coach/consultant in literacy development

WEEKLY READER®
PUBLISHING

Please visit our web site at **www.garethstevens.com.**
For a free catalog describing Gareth Stevens Publishing's list of high-quality books, call 1-800-542-2595 (USA) or 1-800-387-3178 (Canada). Our fax: 877-542-2596

Library of Congress Cataloging-in-Publication Data

Guidone, Lisa M.
    What happens at a museum? / by Lisa M. Guidone.
        p. cm. — (Where people work)
    Includes bibliographical references and index.
    ISBN-10: 0-8368-9276-3   ISBN-13: 978-0-8368-9276-5 (lib. bdg. : alk. paper)
    ISBN-10: 0-8368-9375-1   ISBN-13: 978-0-8368-9375-5 (softcover : alk. paper)
    1. Natural history museums—Juvenile literature. I. Title.
QH70.A1G85   2009
508.075—dc22   2008006093

This edition first published in 2009 by
Weekly Reader® Books
An Imprint of Gareth Stevens Publishing
1 Reader's Digest Road
Pleasantville, NY 10570-7000 USA

Copyright © 2009 by Gareth Stevens, Inc.

Buddy® is a registered trademark of Weekly Reader Corporation. Used under license.

Senior Managing Editor: Lisa M. Herrington
Creative Director: Lisa Donovan
Designer: Alexandria Davis
Photo Coordinator: Charlene Pinckney

All photographs by Richard Hutchings except page 9 and page 21 courtesy of the Yale Peabody Museum of Natural History.

The publisher thanks Vicki Fitzgerald, Marilyn Fox, Joyce Gherlone, Ariel Revan, and Louis Tremblay at the Yale Peabody Museum of Natural History in New Haven, Connecticut, for sharing their expertise and love of dinosaurs.

All rights reserved. No part of this book may be reproduced, stored in a retrieval system, or transmitted in any form or by any means, electronic, mechanical, photocopying, recording, or otherwise, without the prior written permission of the copyright holder.

Printed in the United States of America

1 2 3 4 5 6 7 8 9 10 09 08

BR 508.D75
GUI

Hi, Kids,

I'm Buddy, your Weekly Reader® pal. Have you ever visited a museum? I'm here to show and tell what happens at a natural history museum. So, come on. Turn the page and read along!

JUN 26 2009

GERMANTOWN COMMUNITY LIBRARY
GERMANTOWN, WI 53022

Boldface words appear in the glossary.

There are many types of **museums**. A natural history museum is a place where people learn about the past.

A museum has many **exhibits**. An exhibit shows things for people to see. This exhibit is called the Great Hall of Dinosaurs. Look at all the dinos!

exhibit

Before the dinosaurs come to the museum, workers find and dig up their bones. These bones are very old. They are called **fossils**.

fossil

To get the bones to the museum safely, they are put in a hard material called **plaster**. Museum workers carefully cut open the plaster with a saw.

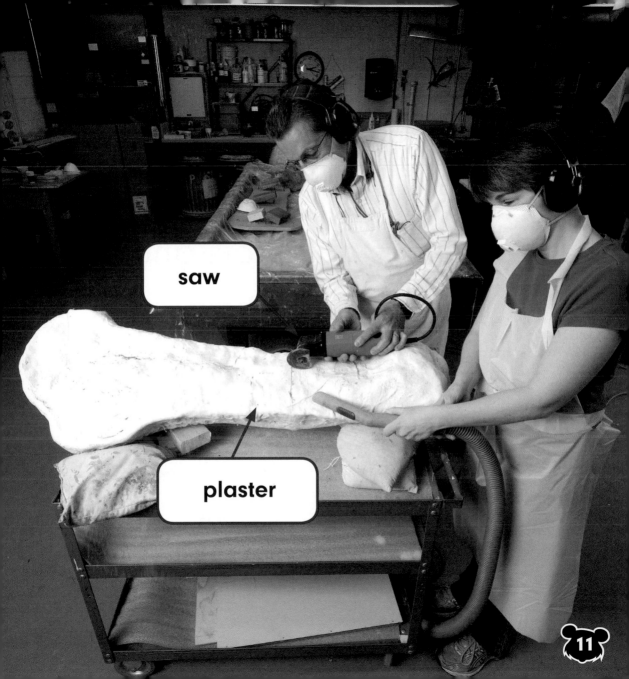

saw

plaster

After the plaster is open,
the workers clean the bone.
They use small tools and
a brush to clear away the
rocks. Later, the workers
study the bone.

tools

brush

Building the dinosaur is like putting together a puzzle. Workers have to fill in the missing parts. They use **molds** to make copies of real bones.

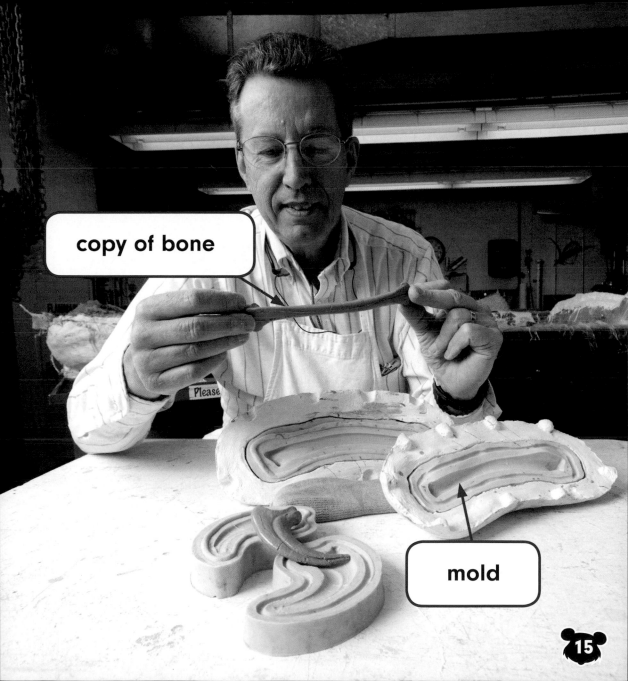

copy of bone

mold

15

Once the dinosaur is built, it is put in an exhibit. People can learn all about the dinosaur.

The Hall of
Mammalian Evolution

Only some of the fossils are shown in exhibits. Other workers take care of the fossils that are not in exhibits.

A **guide** tells visitors about what is in the museum. This guide talks to kids in the Great Hall of Dinosaurs.

guide

 # Glossary

exhibits: things shown in a museum for people to see

fossils: remains of plants and animals from the past, such as dinosaur bones, that are found in the ground

guide: a person who shows and explains things of interest to people visiting a museum

molds: open forms that are filled with a liquid that hardens into an exact copy of a real bone

museums: buildings that show things of interest and value to people who visit

plaster: a material that hardens around something to protect it

🐻 For More Information

Books

Dinosaur Hunters. Richard and Louise Spilsbury (Heinemann, 2007)

Let's Read About Dinosaurs (series). Joanne Mattern (Gareth Stevens Publishing, 2007)

Web Sites

Dinosaurs at Enchanted Learning

www.enchantedlearning.com/themes/dinos.shtml
Find quizzes, activities, and facts about dinosaurs.

Yale Peabody Museum of Natural History

www.peabody.yale.edu/collections/vp/vplab.html
Explore more about how fossil bones are prepared for exhibit.

Publisher's note to educators and parents: Our editors have carefully reviewed these web sites to ensure that they are suitable for children. Many web sites change frequently, however, and we cannot guarantee that a site's future contents will continue to meet our high standards of quality and educational value. Be advised that children should be closely supervised whenever they access the Internet.

 # Index

bones 8, 10, 12, 14

dinosaurs 6, 8, 14, 16, 20

exhibits 6, 16, 18

fossils 8, 18

guide 20

molds 14

museum 4, 6, 8, 10, 20

plaster 10, 12

saw 10

tools 12

About the Author

Lisa M. Guidone works in children's publishing. She has written and edited children's books and magazines for Weekly Reader for nearly eight years. She lives in Trumbull, Connecticut, with her husband, Ryan. She dedicates this book to her new nephew, Anthony, in hopes he shares her love of reading.